Aardvark to Zucchini

Phonetic Alphabet Book

Learn to read with ease

Written by

Joan A. Hentschel

Illustrated by

Suzanne M. Peyer

Aardvark to Zucchini Press, Inc.

West Des Moines, Iowa

Text ©2016 by Joan A. Hentschel
Illustrations ©2016 by Suzanne M. Peyer
Design and layout ©2016 by Aardvark to Zucchini Press, Inc.

All rights reserved. Published in the United States of America by Aardvark to Zucchini Press, Inc., West Des Moines, Iowa.
www.aardvarktozucchini.com

This book may not be reproduced, transmitted, or stored in whole or in part in any form or by any means, electronic or mechanical, including photocopying without the written consent of the publisher. For information regarding permission, contact Aardvark to Zucchini Press.

Hentschel, Joan A.
Aardvark to Zucchini Phonetic Alphabet Book /
Joan A. Hentschel;
Illustrations by Suzanne M. Peyer
ISBN 978-0-692-26242-9
Printed in the United States of America
First Edition

A reader series primer
to teach children to read with ease

Inspired by what could be

———

FOR
The reader
May your letters produce words
that build knowledge.

———

This book is dedicated to my husband Bruce
for his eternal love and support.

I am grateful to Suzanne
for her partnership in creating this book.

Contents

Introduction 1
Instructions 3
    Review Sounds 3
    New Sounds 3
    New Words 4
    Sentences! 5
    Phonetic Alphabet 6
    Aardvark to Zucchini Phonetic Alphabet 7
    Sight Words 8
    Closing Remarks 11
Chapter 1: a, c, n, p, t 15
Chapter 2: b, m, r, s 23
Chapter 3: d, e, o 31
Chapter 4: f, i, l 39
Chapter 5: g, *sh*, *th* 47
Chapter 6: ing, ong, oo 55
Chapter 7: er, h, w 63
Chapter 8: ck, u, ung 71
Chapter 9: *ch*, ir, ur 79
Chapter 10: j, k, y 87
Chapter 11: ang, au, aw 95
Chapter 12: a, silent e 103
Chapter 13: v, x, z 111
Chapter 14: ea, ee, *qu* 119
Chapter 15: o, oa, or 127
Chapter 16: ar, y 135
Chapter 17: ew, u, wh 143
Chapter 18: i, igh, *ph*, kn 151
Chapter 19: ai, ay, oi, oy 159
Chapter 20: *dge*, ou, ow, *tion* 167
Appendix: Exceptions 177

Introduction

Welcome to the A**ar**dv**ar**k to Z*u*cchini **Ph**_o_netic Al**ph**abet B_oo_k, a tool for teaching individuals to read. This teaching method makes reading simple and is appropriate for any age child or adult who has exhibited a desire to read.

This book introduces a unique phonetic alphabet containing the majority of the letter sounds in the English language. The A**ar**dv**ar**k to Z*u*cchini **Ph**_o_netic Al**ph**abet contains aids that enable pupils to know with a mere glance how to pronounce words. Eventually the aids are removed and pupils barely notice their absence.

The book can be used to teach children to read prior to entering kindergarten. The chapters are designed to take no more than 15 minutes of time each day. A new chapter of this book can be introduced each day for 20 days when teaching a quick learner.

With younger pupils, you may spread the chapters out over a longer period of time and may find it helpful to repeat chapters. Some users of this book have found it beneficial to read the book multiple times with their children to strengthen reading ability.

Be sure to read the Instructions section as it contains important details pertaining to this teaching method, including the A**ar**dv**ar**k to Z*u*cchini **Ph**_o_netic Al**ph**abet. The detailed instructions are of equal importance as the phonetic alphabet itself.

I am excited that you and your students are trying this phonetics approach to reading. There is so much promise in your protégés' futures.

Happy Reading!

Instructions

This book increases a child's reading readiness through teacher-student interaction, simplistic presentation of phonetic sounds, and continual reinforcement of mastered sounds.

New letter sounds are introduced and reinforced at a pace that enables the pupil to commit sounds to memory. Each chapter contains the following sections: Review Sounds, New Sounds, New Words, and Sentences. Follow the instructions provided here to maximize the reading benefit from each section in a chapter.

Review Sounds

Each chapter begins with a "Review Sounds" section that reinforces the phonetic sounds introduced in the two preceding chapters. Pronounce these sounds together before proceeding to the "New Sounds" section. If necessary, review the sounds more than once. This section is very important since new readers feel comfortable and develop self-confidence by repeating mastered sounds.

New Sounds

In the "New Sounds" section, the reader is introduced to new phonetic letter sounds. Refer to the phonetic alphabet in this Instructions section before starting each chapter to ensure proper pronunciation of each of these new sounds. Pronounce each of the phonetic sounds together three or four times. When you teach a letter, refrain from referring to the letter by its name. **Refer to the letter by its phonetic sound only!**

New Words

In the "New Words" section, the reader will learn 12 new words that contain the sounds introduced in the chapter. These words are presented twice in this section, un-illustrated and illustrated.

The un-illustrated words are presented first to ensure that pupils are not relying upon images for pronunciation. Slowly pronounce each un-illustrated word together three or four times.

When pronouncing the new words together, consider each letter in a word as a sound part that can stand on its own. You and your pupil are merely connecting the parts. This process is similar to joining two words in a compound word or connecting multiple words to form a sentence. For example, the word "grapevine" can be pronounced as two separate words, "grape" and "vine." When gradually spoken faster in sequence these two words become the single word "grapevine." Similarly, when teaching someone to read letters that create a word, we connect each phonetic sound slowly at first and then gradually speed up that process until the sounds form a word.

New readers benefit from holding the phonetic sounds while gazing at the letters. This process allows the student's brain to connect the letters with the phonetic sounds. Therefore, take time to read the words slowly together. Place your finger under each letter as you and your student pronounce the sounds together. Aim for a continuous flow of sound for each word. Sustain easy-to-hold letters like "s" and "r" to allow your student to approach reading slowly. With hard-to-hold letters such as "p" and "t," you can proceed to the next letter in a word without hesitation.

Following is a pictorial explanation of how to pronounce the word "cat" with your student.

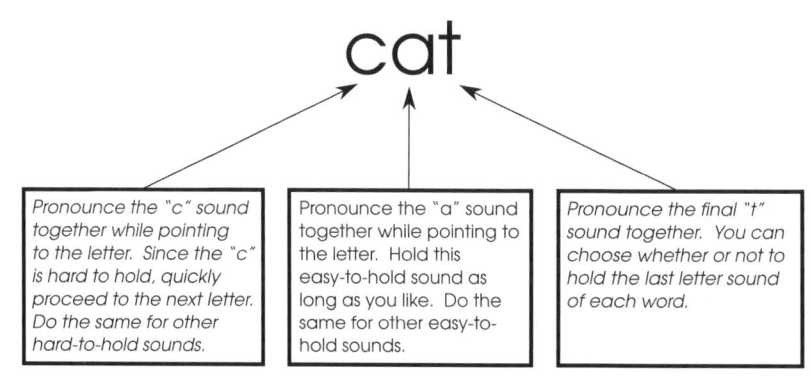

cat

Pronounce the "c" sound together while pointing to the letter. Since the "c" is hard to hold, quickly proceed to the next letter. Do the same for other hard-to-hold sounds.

Pronounce the "a" sound together while pointing to the letter. Hold this easy-to-hold sound as long as you like. Do the same for other easy-to-hold sounds.

Pronounce the final "t" sound together. You can choose whether or not to hold the last letter sound of each word.

Demonstrate this process with the first word in each chapter before engaging your pupil. Then, read each un-illustrated word aloud together several times. The following text is an example of instruction you can provide as you introduce the words.

"Let's read some words formed from the new sounds we have learned! Let's pronounce each word three times together. We will hold some sounds longer than others. Are you ready? Let's read words!"

Each time you repeat a word, together, gradually increase the pace until you pronounce the word smoothly. With increased speed, you will find that your student knows the word. He or she may fill with excitement and shout out the word.

You may wish to offer additional instruction to your student during the pronunciation process. For example, while your student is holding the sound "a" in the word cat you might say, *"Get ready, we are about to proceed to the next letter."* In more complex words, you may tell the student that the next letter is hard to hold, thus together you will continue quickly to the letter that follows.

Once you have pronounced each un-illustrated word three or four times, turn the page and allow the student to read the words again with the aid of illustrations. This exercise is more entertaining for the reader and reinforces reading the new words correctly.

By subtle observation, validate whether your student is successfully learning to read. You can periodically lower your voice to better hear your pupil pronouncing the words. At times, you may resist temptation to be the first to pronounce a letter. You may be surprised to hear your student say the next sound before you do. However, if your pupil does not say the sound immediately, help him or her by initiating the sound so as to encourage, not frustrate. These tips can be used occasionally for assessing progress but should not replace the overall experience of pronouncing and reading together throughout this book.

Sentences!

The "Sentences!" section of each chapter is designed to reinforce the new words learned. These sentences also leverage words learned in previous chapters. To avoid overwhelming the student, only a few sentences are introduced. As you can imagine, reading words for the first time can be challenging. Reading sentences formed from words can be that much more challenging for a new reader. If a reader struggles with the sentences, simply place more emphasis on reading words. If a reader masters the sentences, you may try forming sentences on your own together for added reinforcement.

Phonetic Alphabet

The Aardvark to Zucchini Phonetic Alphabet used in this book is introduced on the following page. Refer to this page for the proper pronunciation of all letters and their combinations. A key to the Aardvark to Zucchini Phonetic Alphabet is that each letter combination has a unique appearance to denote that letter combination's phonetic sound. The letters may be bold, colored, italicized, or underlined for a specific phonetic sound. Thus, students see a unique font within a word based upon the phonetic sound produced by a letter or combination of letters.

Unlike other phonetic approaches, this method retains the original spelling of the word. Review the letters and corresponding sounds of the phonetic alphabet in this Instructions section before you start chapter one. **Remember to refer to each letter by its phonetic sound instead of the letter name as you progress through the book together.**

The words introduced to your pupil throughout in this book were specially chosen because they contain the Aardvark to Zucchini Phonetic Alphabet sounds or similar sounds. There are some words introduced to your pupil herein that contain sounds that are not perfect matches with the Aardvark to Zucchini Phonetic Alphabet sounds. Some examples of these are noted here.

The sound "oo" is introduced as in the word "cool." However, this sound is also used to introduce words such as "wood." The "oo" sound in the word "wood" is a slight variation of the "oo" sound in the word "cool." No attempt is made to differentiate these sounds in this book because children quickly learn that the "oo" combination can make either sound. They will learn to try both sounds when pronouncing words on their own.

Aardvark to Zucchini Phonetic Alphabet

Sound	as in	Sound	as in
a	hat	m	man
a	drank	n	nap
ai	snail	o	mom
ang	hang	o	home
ar	bark	oa	goat
au	autumn	oi	coin
aw	dawn	ong	long
ay	play	oo	loon
b	bat	or	corn
c	cat	ou	cloud
ch	children	ow	cow
ck	truck	oy	royal
d	dot	p	pan
dge	bridge	ph	photon
e	bed	qu	queen
silent e	ate	r	ran
ea	beak	s	sat
ee	beet	sh	fish
er	dinner	t	tap
ew	blew	th	thin
f	fox	tion	elevation
g	gal	u	cluck
h	hamster	u	cucumber
i	split	ung	stung
i	kite	ur	burger
igh	night	v	river
ing	sing	w	wedding
ir	bird	wh	whale
j	jump	x	box
k	kilt	y	yak
kn	knit	y	puppy
l	lad	z	zoo

The long sound "u" is introduced as the sound in the word cucumber. In this book, this sound is used interchangeably to also refer to the long "u" in the word "jute." Similar to the handling of the "oo" sound, no attempt is made to differentiate between the "u" sounds.

The word symphony is introduced later in this book and is pronounced as "seem-foa-nee." Although this is not a perfect match of phonetic sounds for this word, the subtle differences are barely noticed when you pronounce the words faster. The same is true when the word octopus is introduced. For both of these words and others, the closest A**ar**dv**ar**k to Z**u**cchini **Ph**onetic Al**ph**abet sound was chosen to illustrate the pronunciation.

Sight Words

Two sight words - "a" and "the" - are used throughout this book. Before starting chapter one, these two sight words should be taught to your pupil.

You can use the following two pages to teach these sight words. Practice the words by pronouncing "a" or "the" and then say the name of the animal that follows. Explain to your pupil that these words will be memorized and will always be the same color throughout the book.

These sight words are reinforced in chapter one in the "Sight Words" section that appears in lieu of the "Review Sounds" section. Additional sight words are introduced in the appendix of this book.

Important Note:

In chapter one, the sight word "a" is reviewed and the short "a" sound is introduced. As noted in the Phonetic Alphabet section, the short "a" sound takes the sound of the "a" in hat and is denoted in black. It is critical that you verbally communicate the distinction to your pupil between the word "a" and the short "a" sound. These two sounds will be distinguished by their unique colors.

Sight Words

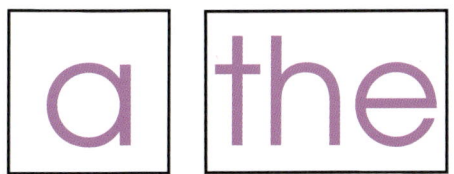

a

a

a

a | the

Sight Words

the

the

the

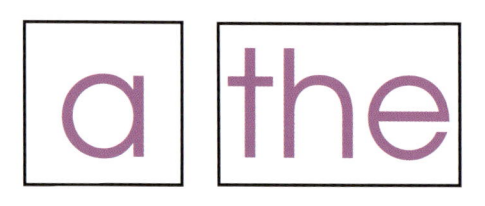

a | the

Closing Remarks

You will find that the phonetic alphabet does not include all sounds. There is no need to fret about this. These sounds are intentionally omitted because they are less frequent in the English language or they are simple derivatives of similar sounds. Your pupil's amazing brain will learn omitted sounds with ease based merely on this primer course in reading.

Capital letters are not taught in this book although they are used in sentences throughout. New readers will generally learn these letters in context, as several capital letters look similar to the lower case letters.

A linguist would point out that some phonetic sounds presented in this book are actually a combination of phonetic sounds, such as "ing." A linguist might also argue that some phonetic sounds are not unique, such as "er," "ir," and "ur." My response is, "Both observations are correct, yet let's build a bridge together to cross safely over that concern." The English language lacks a term for the jump-start approach that I have created here. I have chosen to use "phonetic alphabet" as the best term to describe this expedient way to teach individuals to read. Later in life, students can learn the unique phonetic sounds if they are so inclined. If they are reading from an early age, which is precisely what this book is designed to achieve, such scholars will be more inclined to learn the finer constructs of the English language. Together, those who teach preciseness of the English language and those who jump start reading with a demonstrated approach such as that contained herein will achieve a higher level of literacy for all individuals worldwide.

I hope you and your students will appreciate the simplicity of this phonetic approach.

Good luck! Enjoy!

Joan Hentschel

...Remember, as you journey into the chapters of this book, refer to each letter by its phonetic sound rather than by name. This hint will accelerate the reading process. ...

Chapter 1

Sight Words

a

the

_____

New Sounds

a c n p t

New Words

act	nap
ant	pan
apt	pant
can	tan
cap	tap
cat	tat

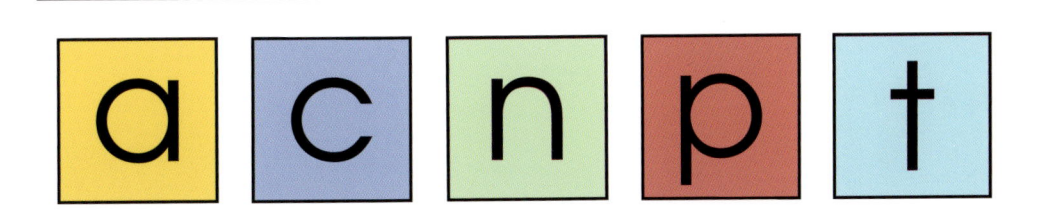

a c n p t

act

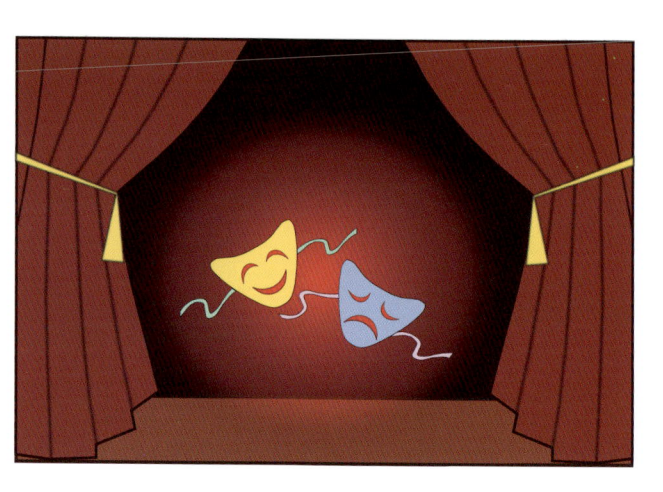

ant

apt

| a | c | n | p | t |

can can't

cap

cat

| a | c | n | p | t |

nap

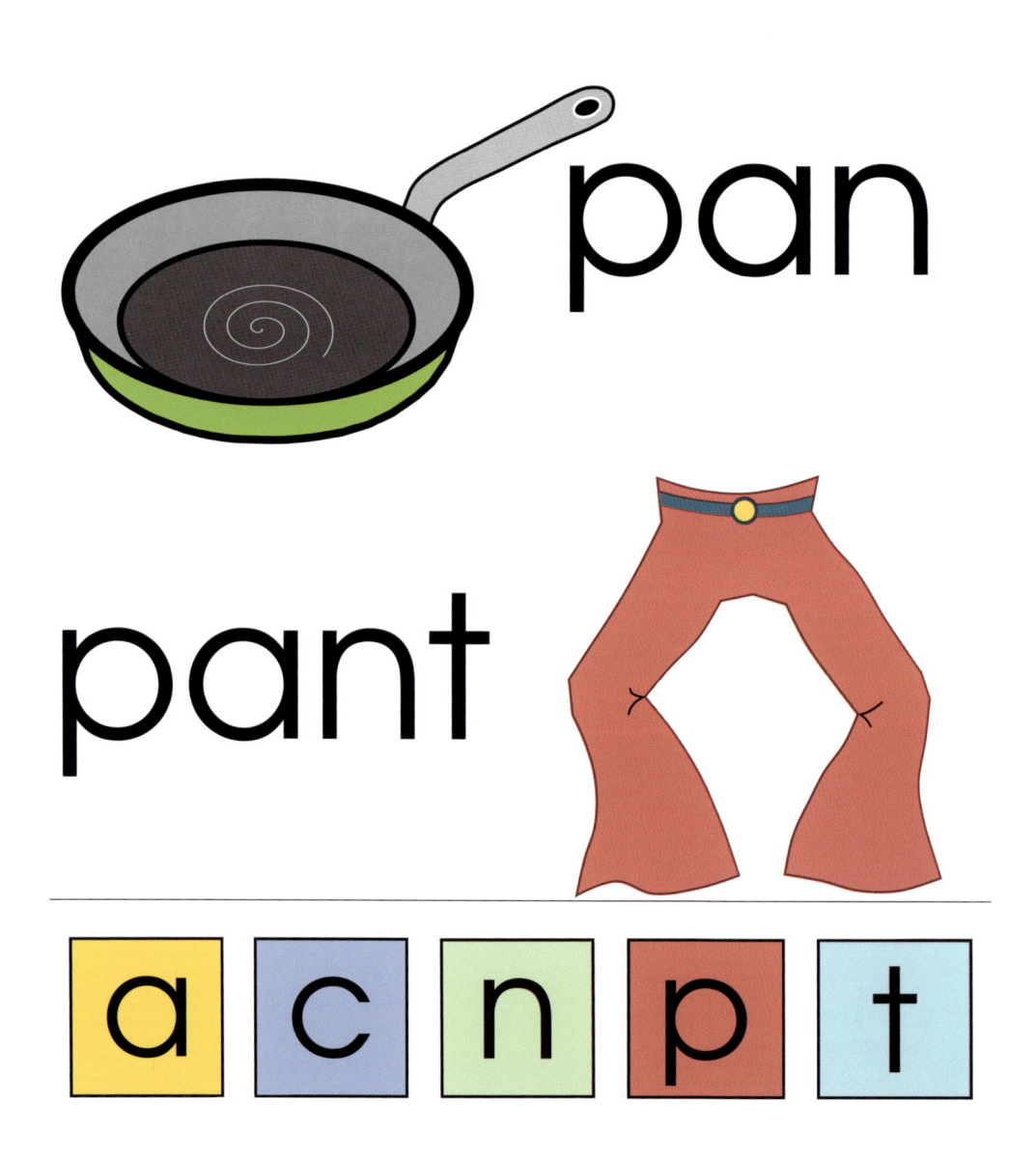

pan

pant

a c n p t

tan

tap

tat

a c n p t

Sentences!

The tan cat can nap.

Can a cat tap?

Can the ant act?

Chapter 2

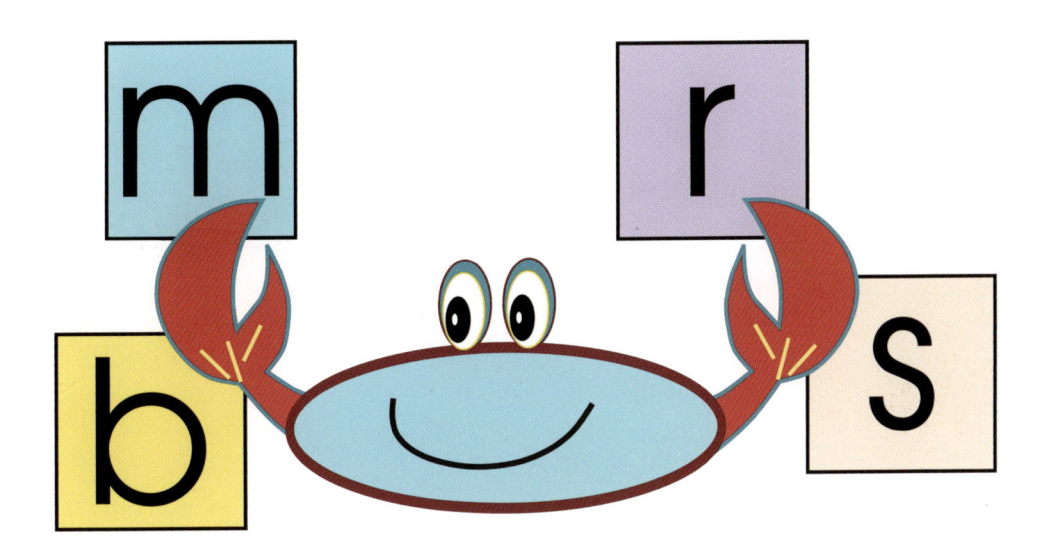

Review Sounds

a c n p t

_____

New Sounds

b m r s

New Words

banana	map
bat	mat
cab	ran
camp	sat
crab	snap
man	strap

b m r s

banana

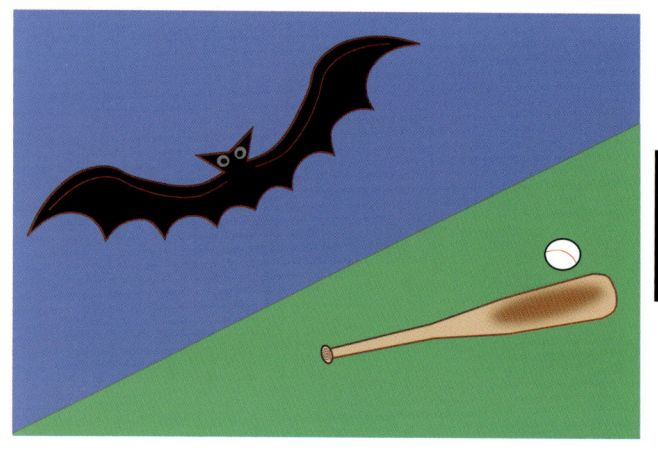

bat

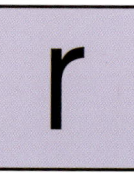

cab

| b | m | r | s |

camp

crab

man

b m r s

27

map

mat

ran

| b | m | r | s |

28

sat

snap

strap

| b | m | r | s |

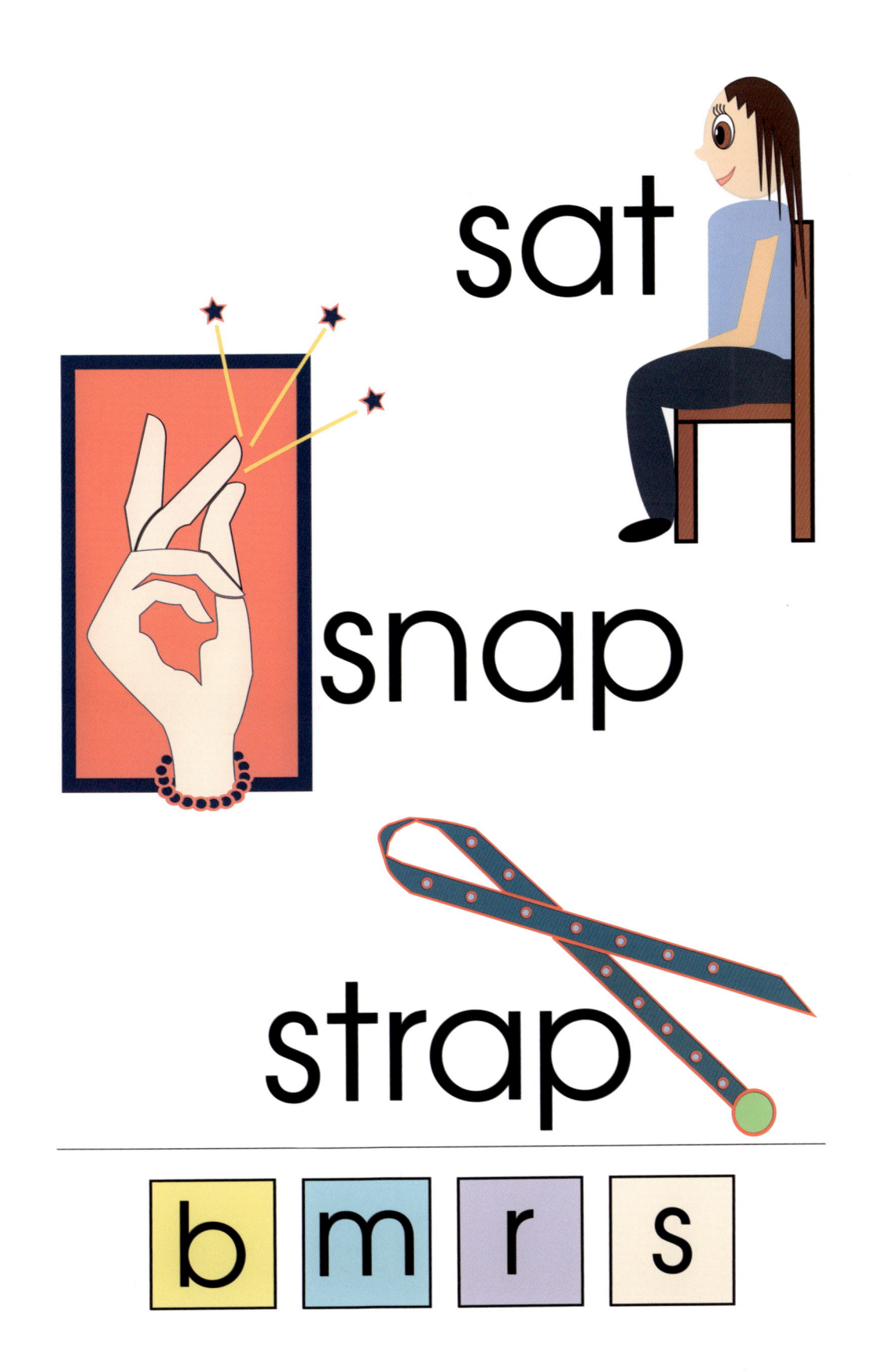

Sentences!

A man ran a camp.

A crab ran a cab.

Ants sat. Cats sat.

Chapter 3

Review Sounds

a c n p t

b m r s

___

New Sounds

d e o

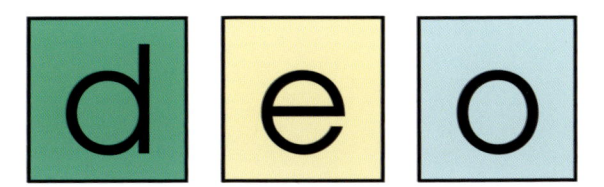

New Words

bed	pond
connect	red
dot	sad
mom	sand
pad	ten
pen	tot

d e o

bed

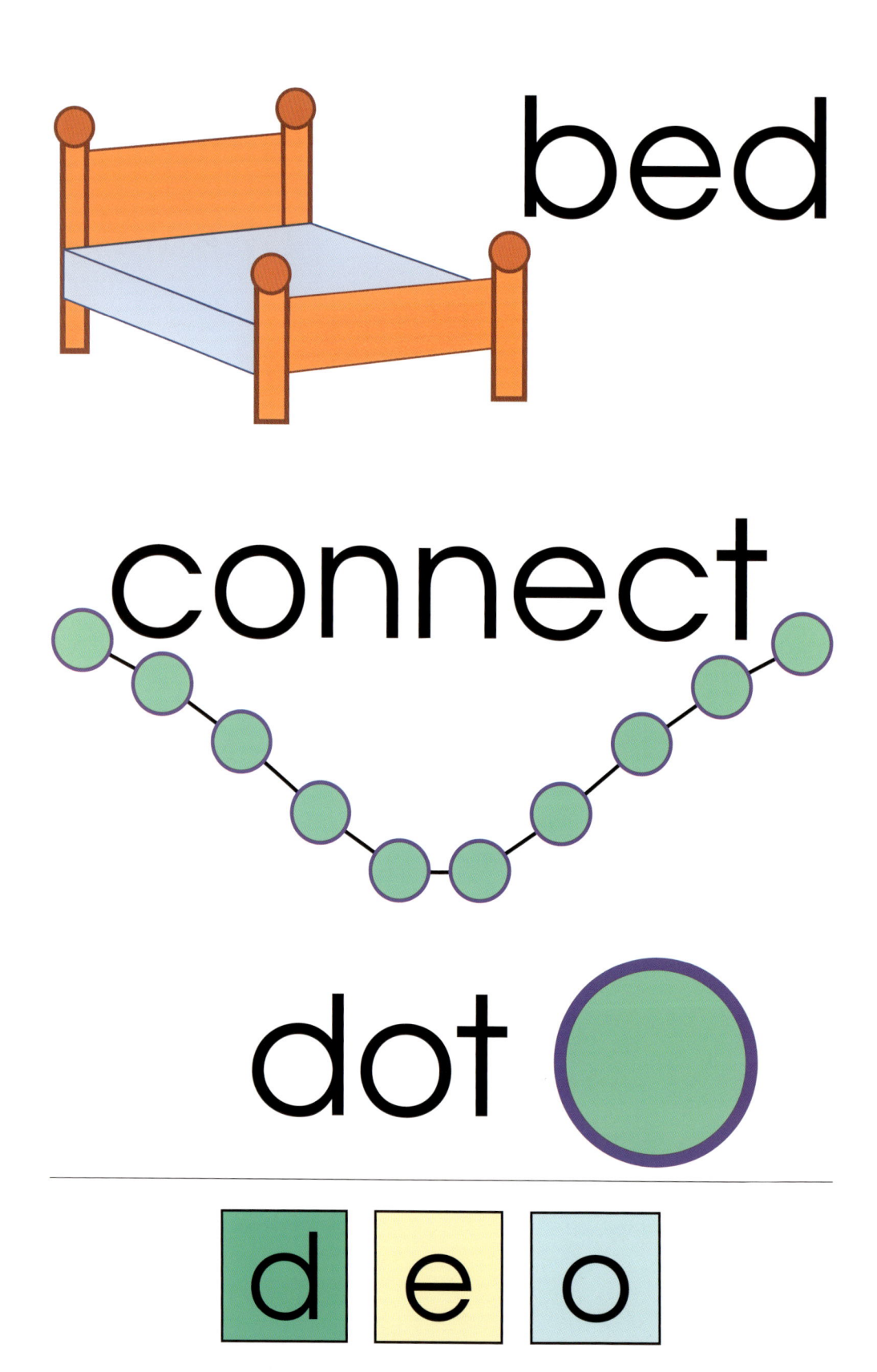

connect

dot

d e o

mom

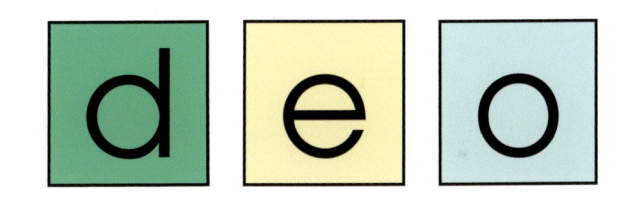

pad

pen

d e o

pond

red

sad

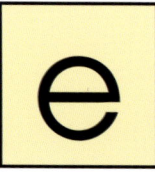

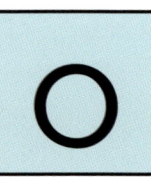

| d | e | o |

sand

ten

tot

d e o

Sentences!

A sad crab sat on a pad.

Mom and tot crab sat on a red bed.

Chapter 4

Review Sounds

b m r s

d e o

———

New Sounds

f i l

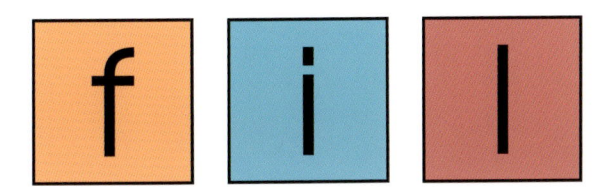

New Words

fell	raft
flan	slept
flip flops	smell
frond	split
lad	stilts
plant	trip

f i l

fell

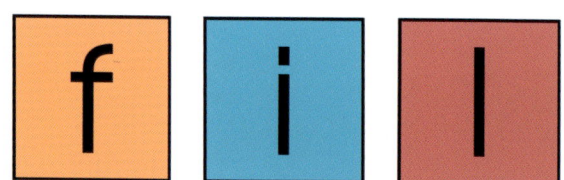

flan

flip

flops

f i l

frond

lad plant

| f | i | l |

raft

slept

smell

| f | i | l |

split

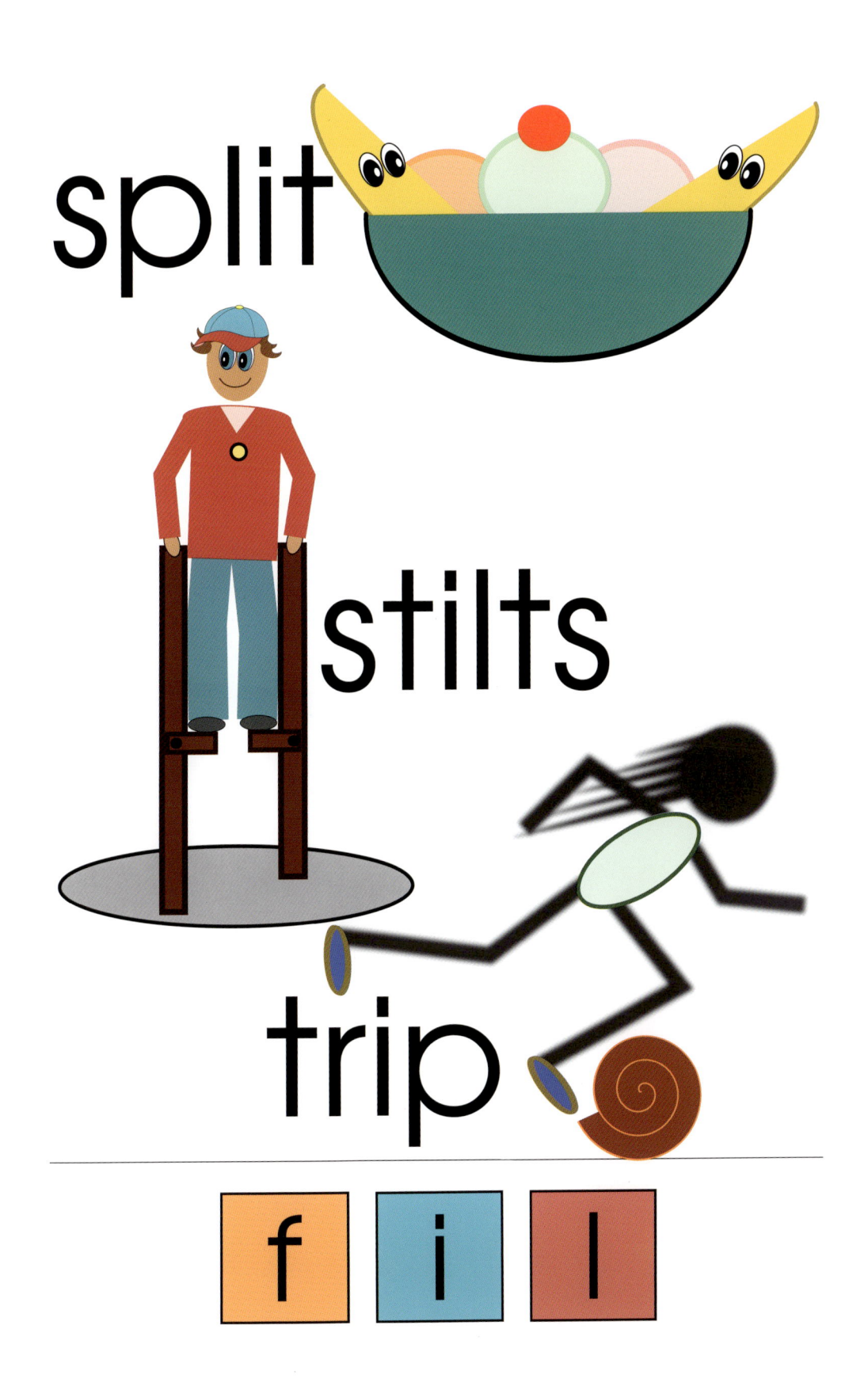

stilts

trip

| f | i | l |

45

Sentences!

Ten ants smell a man's flan.

A lad fell from stilts on a banana split.

Chapter 5

Review Sounds

d e o

f i l

_____

New Sounds

g *sh* *th*

New Words

ba**th**	ma**th**
big	pa**th**
da**sh**	pig
dep**th**	**sh**rimp
fi**sh**	ten**th**
gal	**th**in

g **sh** **th**

ba**th**

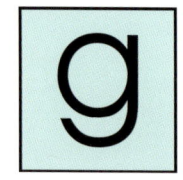

big

da**sh**

| g | *sh* | *th* |

dep*th*

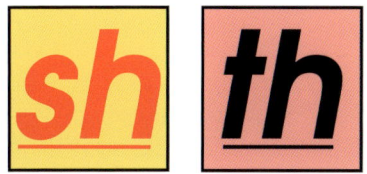

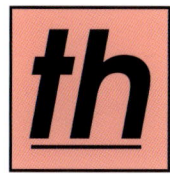

fi*sh*

gal

g *sh* *th*

ma_**th**_ 2+8=10

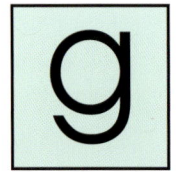

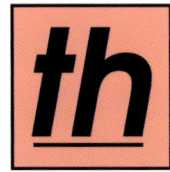

pa_**th**_

pig

| g | *sh* | **th** |

shrimp

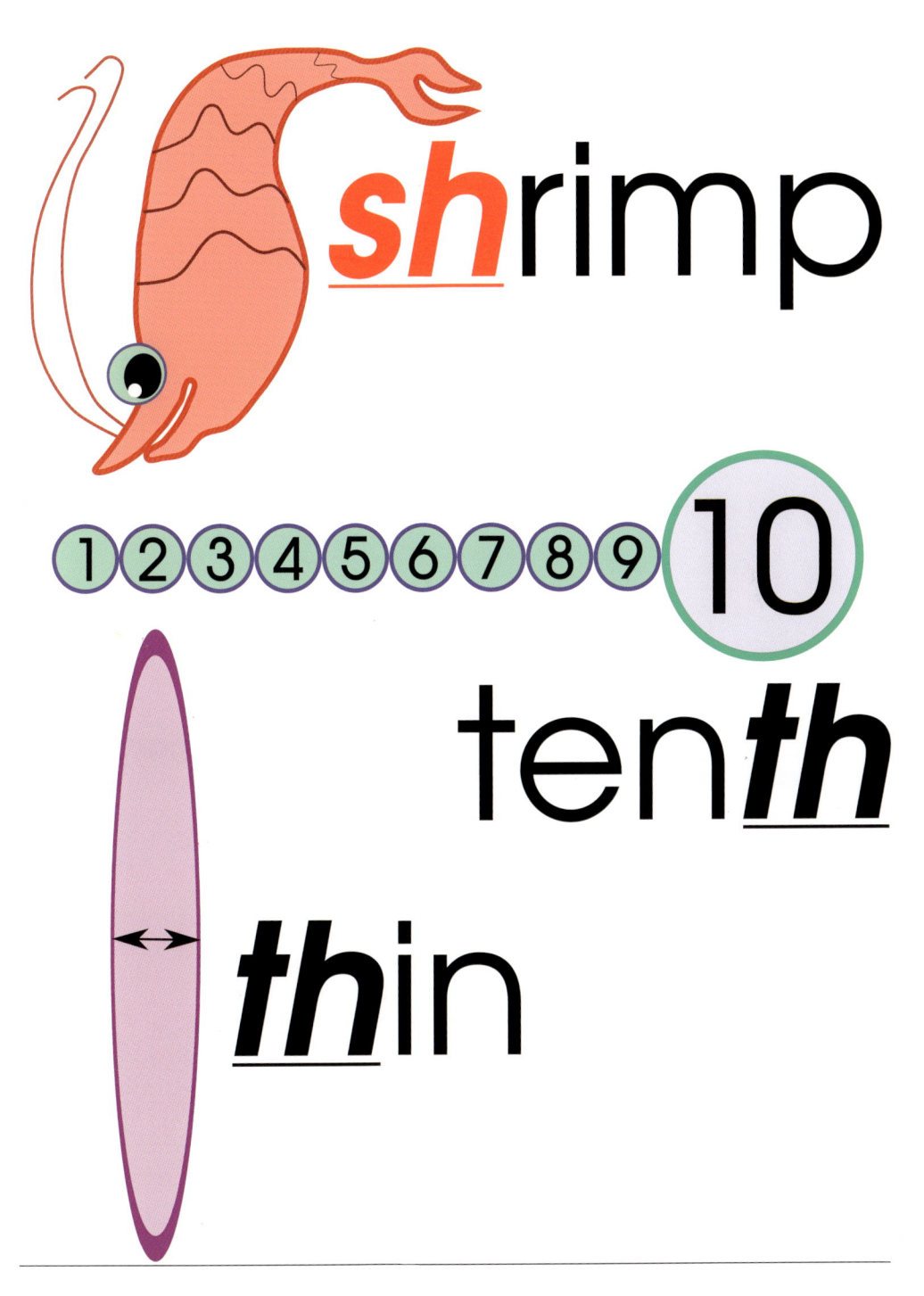

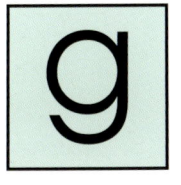

ten**th**

thin

g | *sh* | *th*

Sentences!

A **th**in gal is on a pa**th**.

On the pa**th** is a pig ba**th**.

A **sh**rimp did ma**th**.

Chapter 6

ing ong oo

Review Sounds

f i l

g *sh* *th*

———

New Sounds

ing ong oo

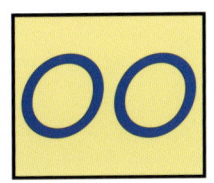

New Words

baboon	mashing
balloon	moon
boo	raccoon
drifting	singing
long	song
loon	strong

ing ong oo

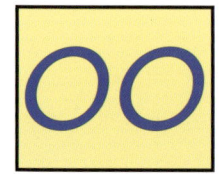

baboon

balloon

boo

| ing | ong | oo |

drift**ing**

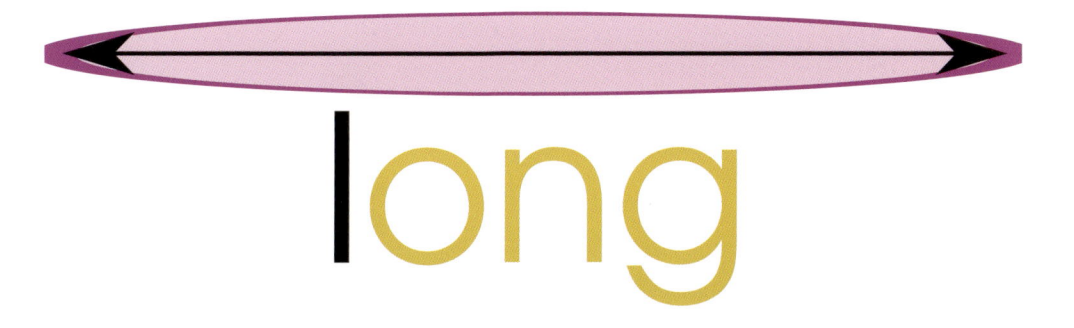

long

loo**n**

ing ong oo

ma**sh**ing

moon

raccoon

ing ong oo

singing

song

strong

ing ong oo

Sentences!

A loon is singing a song.

The balloon is drifting.

A strong baboon naps.

Chapter 7

Review Sounds

g *sh* **th**

ing ong oo

_____

New Sounds

er h w

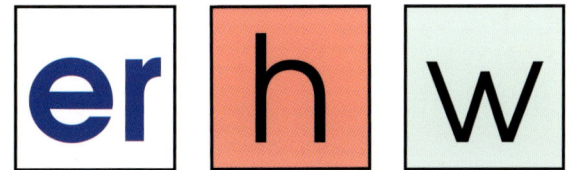

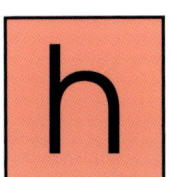

New Words

dinn**er**	sw*oo***sh**
hamst**er**	wedd**ing**
hen	w**ing**s
hilltop	wint**er**
holl**er**	wombat
sw*oo*p	w*oo*ds

er | **h** | **w**

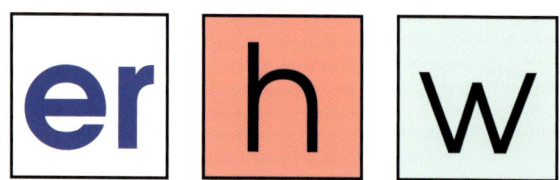

dinn**er**

hamst**er**

hen

| er | h | w |

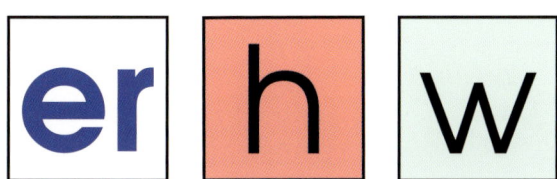

hilltop

holler

swoop

| er | h | w |

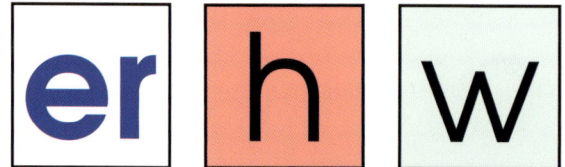

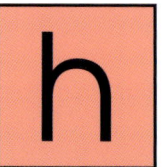

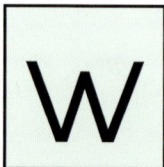

swoosh

wedding

wings

| er | h | w |

winter

wombat

woods

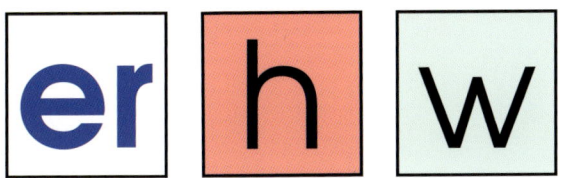

| er | h | w |

Sentences!

Hamsters had a winter wedding.

Raccoons swooshed from the hilltop.

Chapter 8

Review Sounds

ing　ong　oo

er　h　w

_____

New Sounds

ck　u　ung

New Words

black   ladder rungs

bud   sack

cluck   shack

duckling   sprung

flung   sun

grub   truck

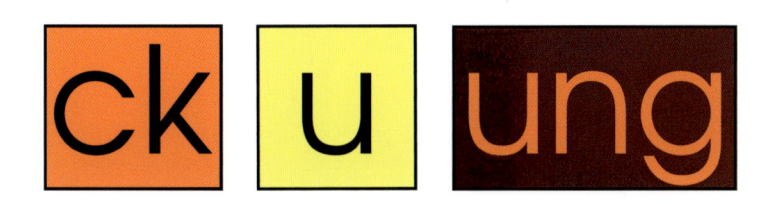

ck **u** **ung**

black

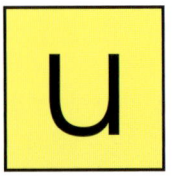

bud

cluck

ck u ung

duckl**ing**

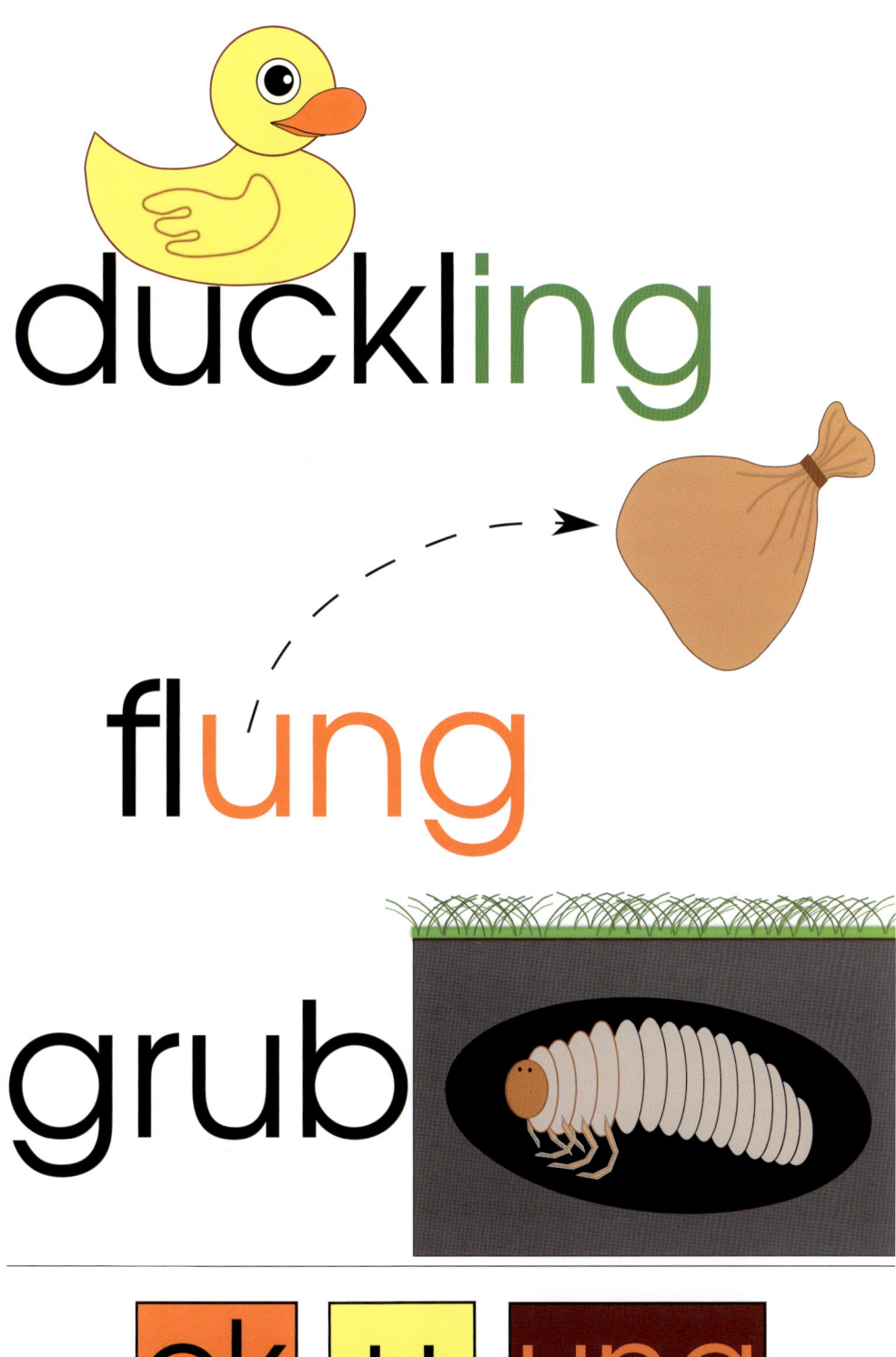

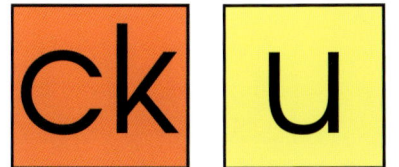

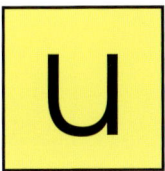

fl**ung**

grub

ck | u | ung

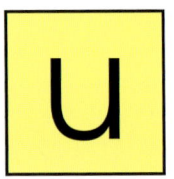

ladd**er** rungs

sack

*sh*ack

| ck | u | ung |

spr**ung**

sun

truck

ck u ung

Sentences!

Spring has sprung.

Hens cluck from a red truck and ladder rungs.

Chapter 9

Review Sounds

er h w

ck u ung

_____

New Sounds

<u>ch</u> ir ur

New Words

bird   dirt

burger   girl

children   munch

chips   scratch

chirps   turf

curb   turn

| ch | ir | ur |

b**ir**d

b**ur**ger

children

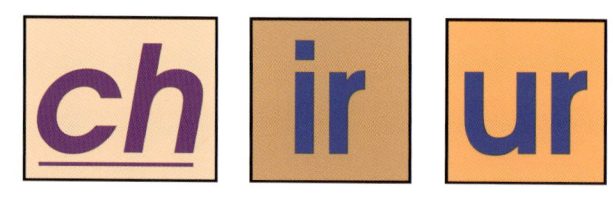

| **ch** | **ir** | **ur** |

chips

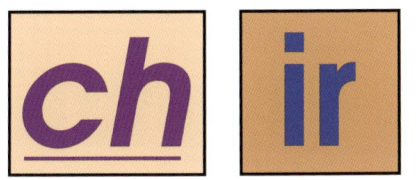

chirps

c**ur**b

| ch | ir | ur |

83

dirt

girl

munch

| ch | ir | ur |

chicken

scrat**ch**

t**ur**f

t**ur**n

ch | **ir** | **ur**

Sentences!

A b**ird** **_ch_**irps.

_Ch_ildren mun**_ch_** on **_ch_**ips and b**ur**g**e**rs.

A g**ir**l t**ur**ns and trips.

Chapter 10

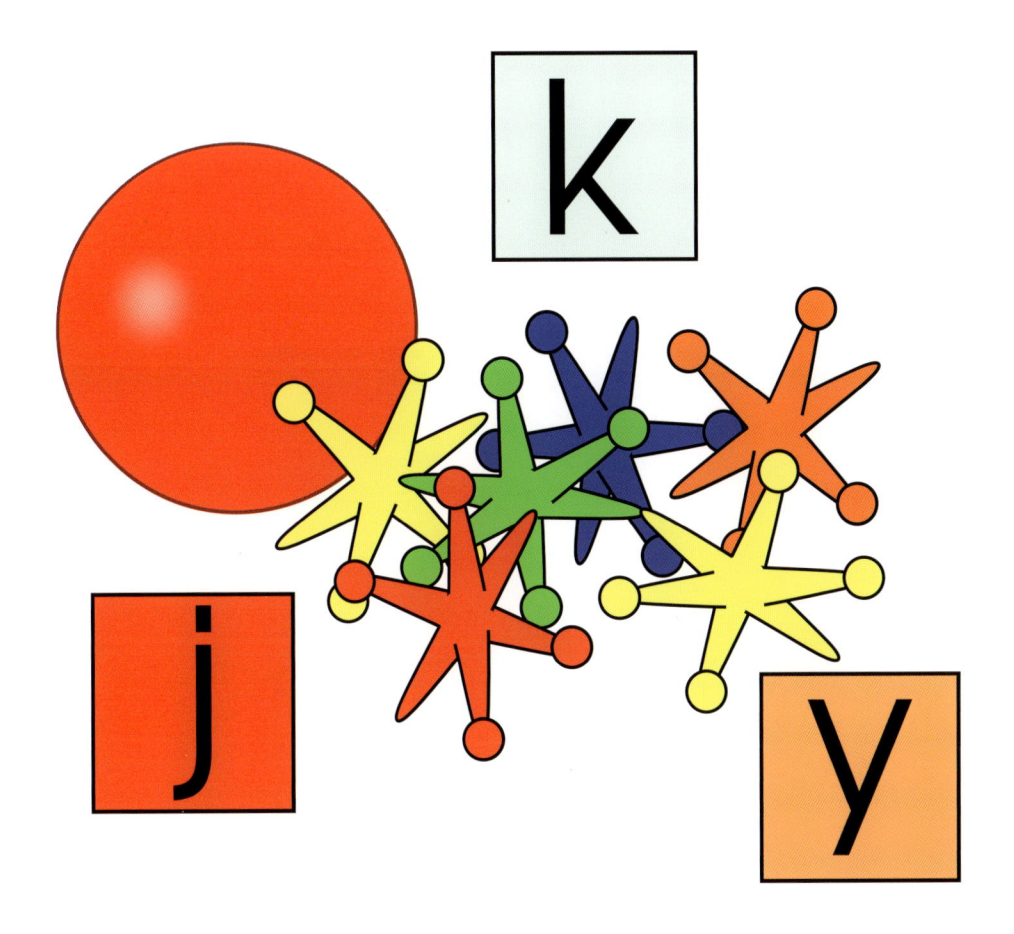

Review Sounds

ck u ung

ch ir ur

———

New Sounds

j k y

New Words

basket	kilt
jacket	milk
jacks	sk**ir**t
jitt**er**bug	yak
jog	yam
jump	yell

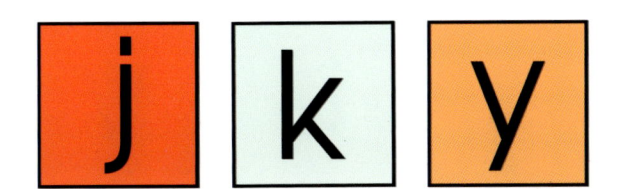

j k y

basket

jacket

jacks

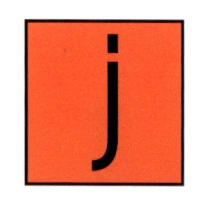

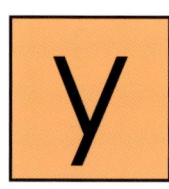

| j | k | y |

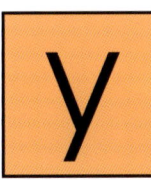

jitt**er**bug

jog

jump

j　k　y

kilt

milk

skirt

| j | k | y |

yak

yam

yell

j k y

Sentences!

A man in a kilt yells, "Yak milk and yams!"

A girl jumps.

Bugs jitterbug.

Chapter 11

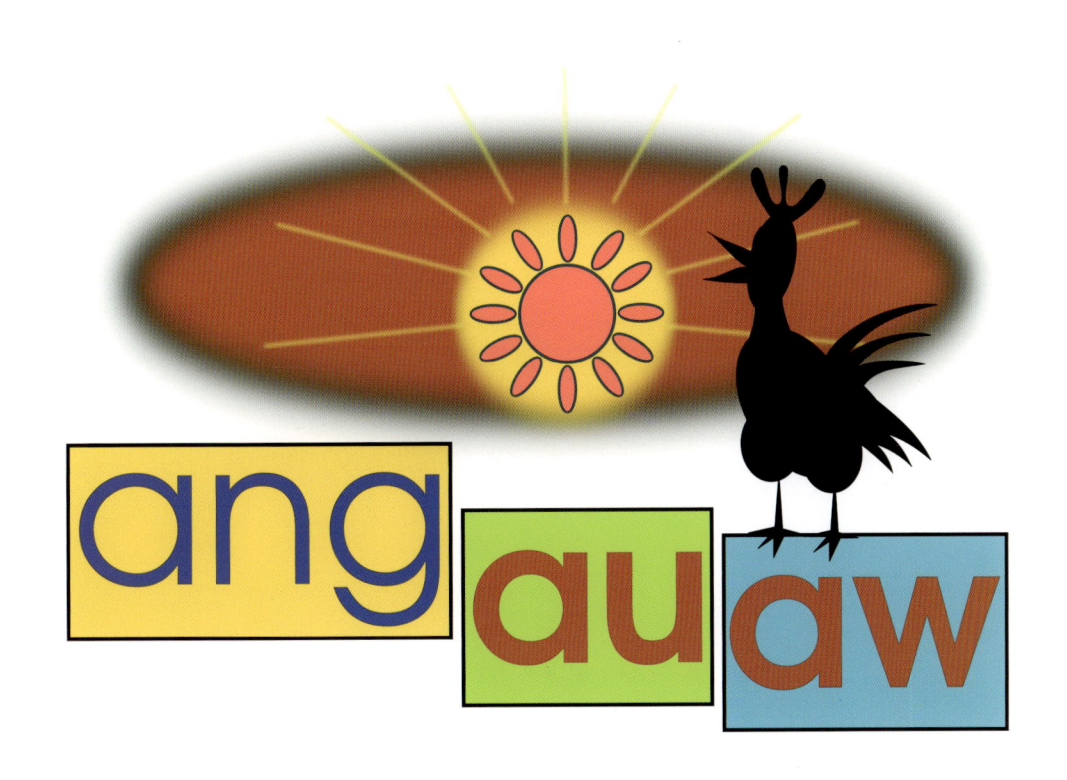

ang au aw

Review Sounds

ch ir ur

j k y

_____

New Sounds

ang au aw

New Words

autumn   haunches

dawn   haunted

fawn   hawk

gaunt   sang

gawk   sprang

hang   swang

ang au aw

autumn

dawn

fawn

| ang | au | aw |

gaunt

gawk

hang

ang　au　aw

haunted

haunches

hawk

| ang | au | aw |

s**ang**

spr**ang**

sw**ang**

ang **au** **aw**

Sentences!

It was dawn in a haunted woods.

A cat sat on its haunches.

A hawk sang.

Chapter 12

a silent e

Review Sounds

j k y

ang au aw

_____

New Sounds

a̲ silent e

New Words

ate grape

bake late

cake milk shake

crate paper

drank plate

gate shipmate

a silent e

ate

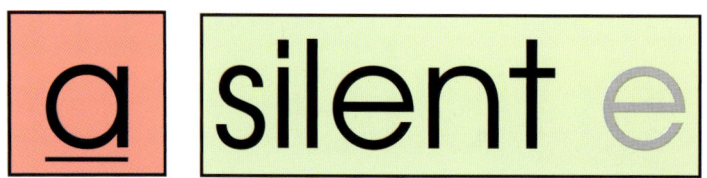

bake

cake

a silent e

crate

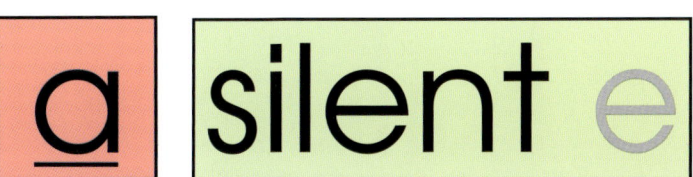

drank

gate

a silent e

gr<u>a</u>pe

l<u>a</u>te

milk s<u>h</u><u>a</u>ke

<u>a</u> silent e

pap**er**

pl**a**t*e*

shipmat*e*

a silent *e*

Sentences!

The **sh**ipmate baked the cake.

Children ate grapes on a crate.

Chapter 13

Review Sounds

ang au aw

a silent e

_____

New Sounds

v x z

New Words

box	graze
exhibit	river
flax	serve
fox	travel
gazelle	zigzag
gravel	zoo

V X Z

box

grazing gazelles

exhibit

flax

v x z

fox

gazelle

gravel

v x z

gr_a_ze

riv**er**

s**er**ve

| v | x | z |

travel

banana camp cab

zig zag

zoo

| v | x | z |

Sentences!

A gazelle grazes on flax at the river.

Children travel at the zoo.

Chapter 14

Review Sounds

a̲ silent e

v x z

_____

New Sounds

e̲a e̲e qu

New Words

banquet

beak

beans

beet

beetles

green

leeks

peacock

peas

queen

quilt

squid

banquet

beak

beans

ea ee qu

beet

beetles

green

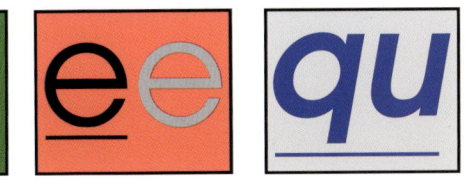

ea ee qu

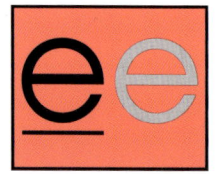

l**ee**ks

p**ea**cock

p**ee**as

ea ee qu

124

queen

quilt

squid

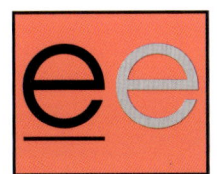

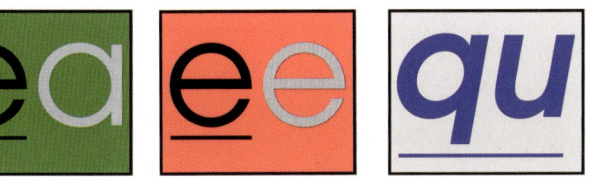

ea ee qu

125

Sentences!

A **_qu_**een held a b_a_nq**_u_**et.

A s**_qu_**id s**_er_**ves be_a_ns, be_e_ts, p_e_as, and le_e_ks.

A p_e_acock _a_te be_e_tles.

Chapter 15

Review Sounds

v   x   z

e̲a   e̲e   *qu*

_____

New Sounds

o̲   o̲a   *or*

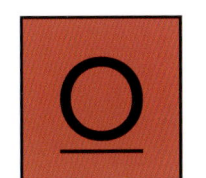

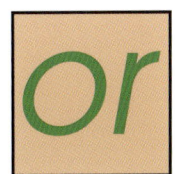

New Words

bloat	horns
coat	horse
corn	road
croak	rode
goat	stone
home	toad

o oa or

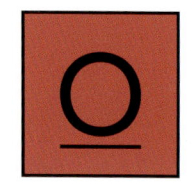

bloat toad

coat

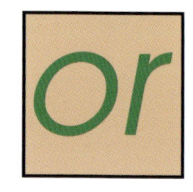

corn

o o a or

croak croak

cr**o**ak

g**o**at

h**o**me

o oa or

h**or**ns

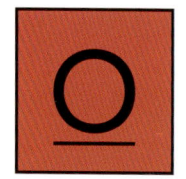

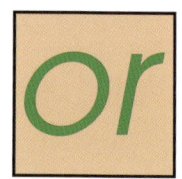

h**or**se

r**o**ad

o | o | or

r<u>o</u>de

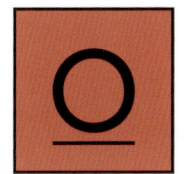

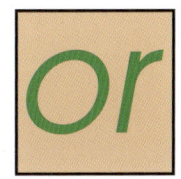

st<u>o</u>ne

t<u>o</u>ad

| <u>o</u> | <u>o</u>a | or |

Sentences!

A man rode home on a stone road.

A horned goat ate corn.

A bloat toad croaked.

Chapter 16

ar y

Review Sounds

e̲a   e̲e   **qu**

o̲   o̲a   *or*

―――――

New Sounds

ar   y̲

New Words

bark

candy

card

charmer

harmonica

march

parade

pony

puppy

queasy

sharply

tardy

ar y

bark

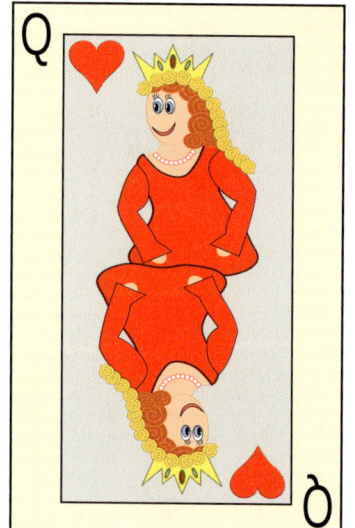

candy

card

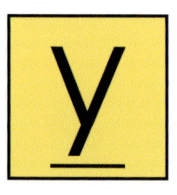

ar y

charmer

harmonica

march

ar y

p**ar**ad_e_

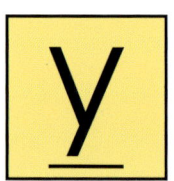

p_o_ny

puppy

ar   y

queasy

sharply

tardy

ar y

Sentences!

The **har**monica band led a p**ar**ade.

A sn_ak_e was **qu**e_a_s_y_.

The p_o_n_y_ was t**ar**d_y_.

Chapter 17

BLUE SEA NEWS

Whelk reports new jewel

Wanda Whelk is broadcasting a treasure trove in the depths of the sea. She reports the discovery of a rare jewel that has not been produced by an oyster. Four invertebrate and one vertebrate species are now traveling the depths in search of the fortune.

Jute net alert!

Narwhal Nelly got her long tooth stuck in yet another jute net. Thanks to the beluga pod, she cruises the sea once again.

Amazing blowhole

Eddie the blue whale blew from a new record low, 100 m below sea level. Way to go Eddie!

ew   u   wh

Review Sounds

o̲ o̲a *or*

ar y̲

_____

New Sounds

*e*w u̲ wh

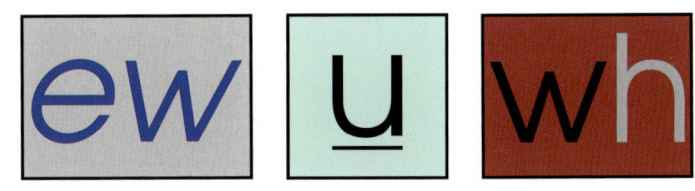

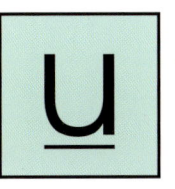

New Words

beluga narwhal

blew news

blue octopus

cucumber whale

jewel whelk

jute whistle

ew u wh

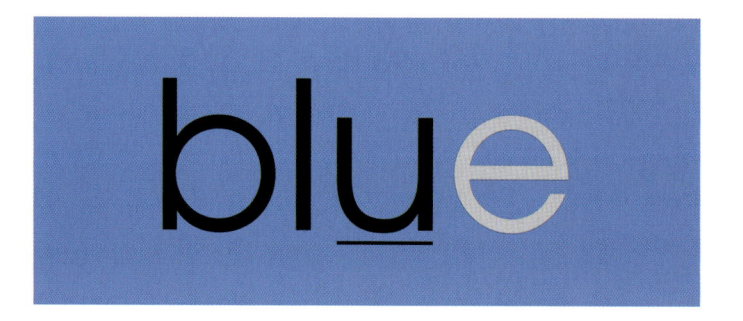

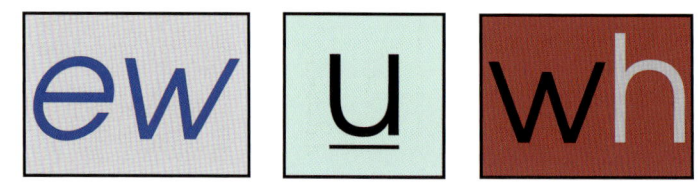

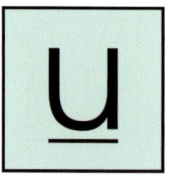

bel_u_ga

bl*ew*

bl_u_e

ew | u | wh

cucumb**er**

jewel

jute

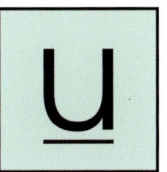

| ew | u | wh |

n**ar**whal

BLUE SEA NEWS
Whelk reports new jewel
Wanda the whelk is broadcasting a treasure trove at the bottom of the sea. She reports that a rare jewel has been discovered, which has not been created by an oyster. Four invertebrates and one vertebrate are now traveling the depth for his fortune.

Narwhal stuck in jute net
Nelly the narwhal got her long tooth stuck in yet another jute net. Thanks to the beluga pod, she cruises the sea once again.

Amazing blowhole
Eddie the blue whale blew his stack from a new record low, 100 m below sea level. Way to go Eddie!

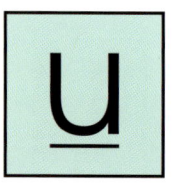

news

octop_u_s

| ew | _u_ | wh |

wh<u>a</u>le

whelk

whistle

| <u>e</u>w | <u>u</u> | wh |

Sentences!

The blue whale blew from the depths of the sea.

A whelk sang of a jewel.

Chapter 18

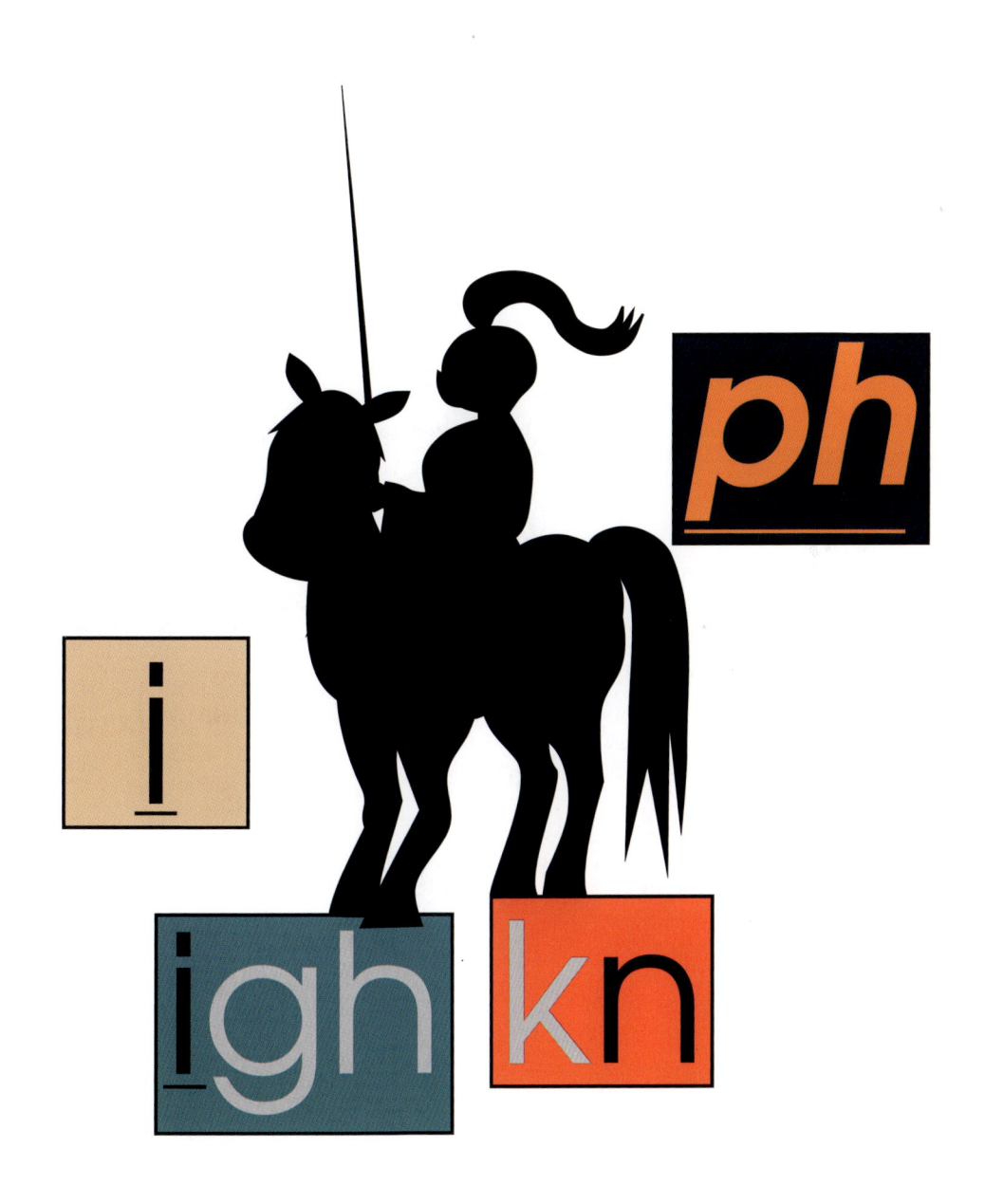

Review Sounds

ar y̲

e̲w u̲ wh

___

New Sounds

i̲ i̲gh kn ***ph***

New Words

frightening lightning

kite

line

kneel

night

knight

photon

knit

symphony

knot

white

i igh kn ph

frightening

kite

kneel

i | igh | kn | ph

kn_i_gh_t

knit

knot

_i_ _igh_ **kn** **_ph_**

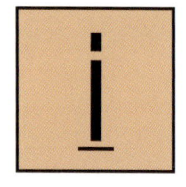

l_ightning

l_ine

n_ight

| i_ | _igh | kn | _ph_ |

photon

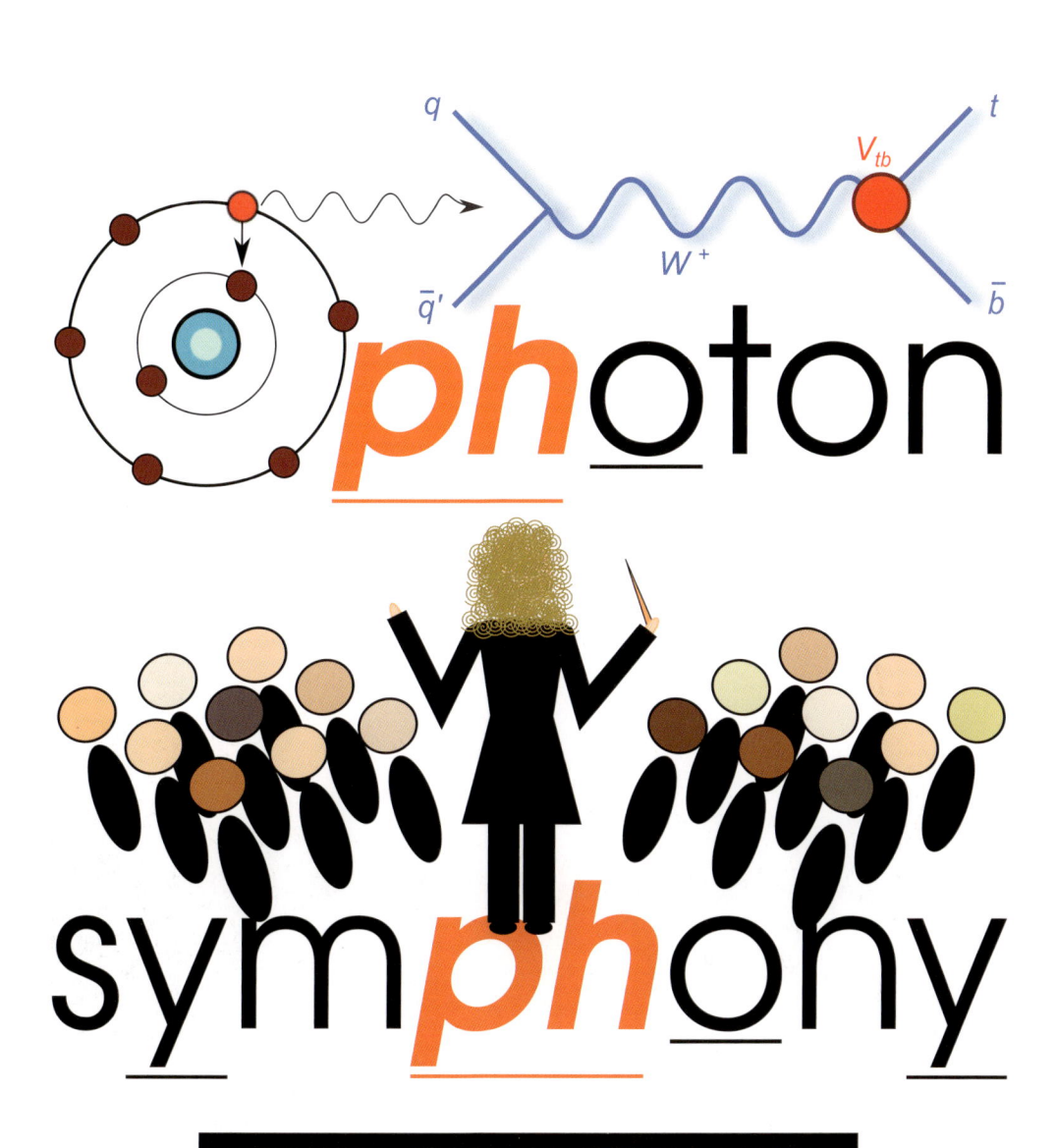

sym**ph**ony

white

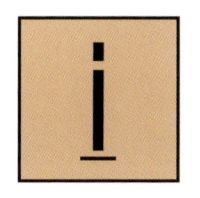

i | igh | kn | **ph**

Sentences!

A knight flew a kite in the night.

Photons sprang from the white lightning.

Chapter 19

Review Sounds

ew u wh

i igh kn *ph*

———

New Sounds

ai ay **oi** **oy**

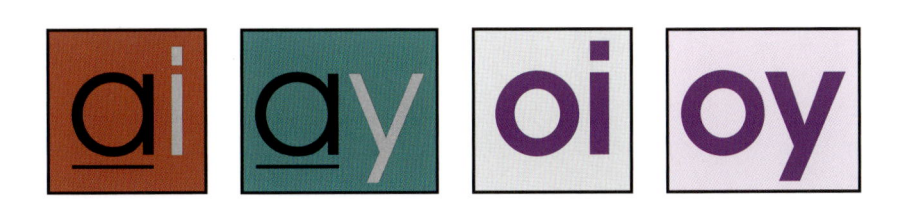

New Words

bay

coil

coins

gargoyle

hay

oink

oyster

play

royal

snail

tail

train

ai ay oi oy

b__a__y

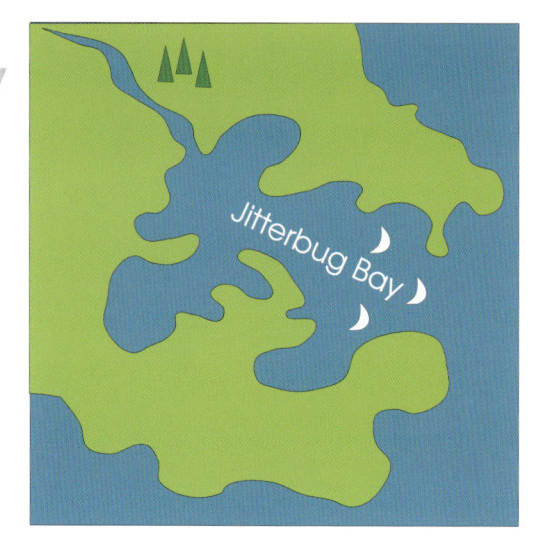

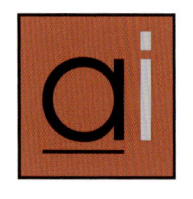

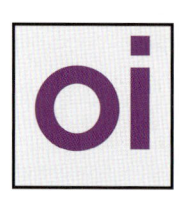

Jitterbug Bay

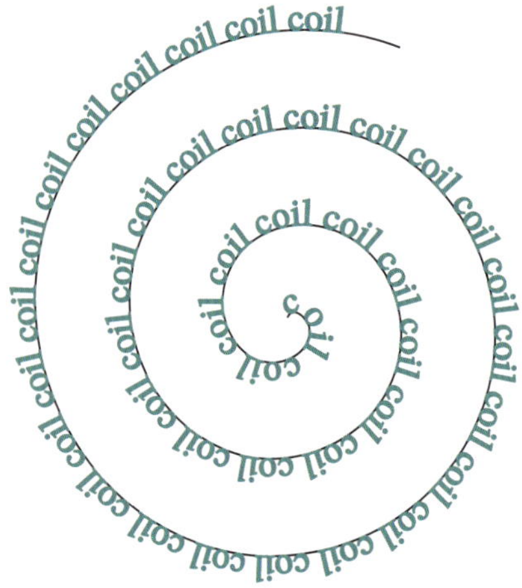

coil

coins

ai ay oi oy

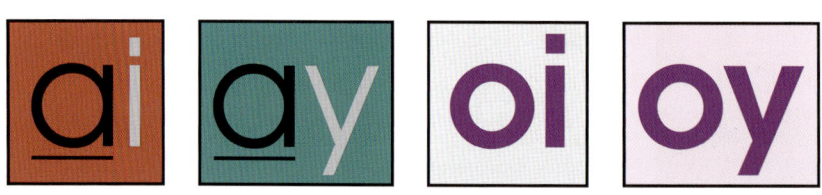

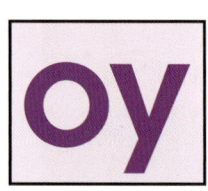

gargoyle

hay

oink oink

oink

| ai | ay | oi | oy |

oyster

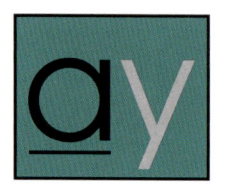

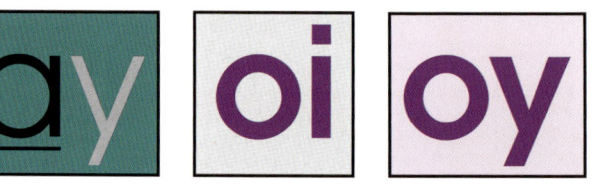

play

royal

ai ay oi oy

sn_a_il

t_a_il

tr_a_in

ai ay oi oy

Sentences!

A tr**a**in travels wi**th** **oy**st**e**rs and j**ew**els.

Pigs **oi**nk and pl**a**y in the h**a**y c**ar**.

Chapter 20

Review Sounds

i̱ i̱gh kn *ph*

a̱i a̱y oi oy

___

New Sounds

dge ou ow *tion*

New Words

badge

bridge

brown

cloud

constellation

cow

elevation

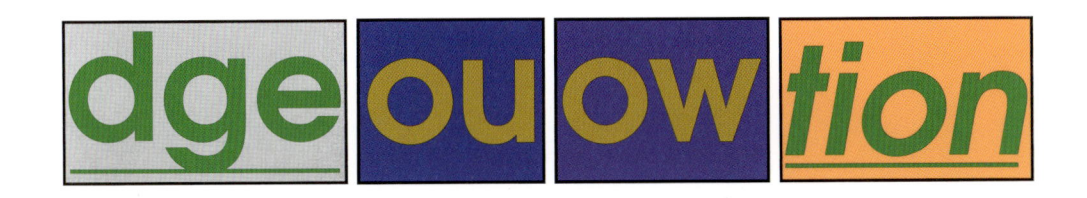

mountain

plow

reflection

ridge

sound

dge ou ow tion

ba**dge**

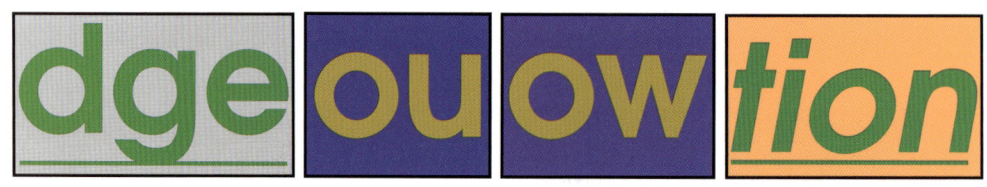

bri**dge**

br**ow**n

| **dge** | **ou** | **ow** | *tion* |

cloud

constella*tion*

cow

| dge | ou | ow | *tion* |

eleva**tion**

mountain

1200 m

plow

| dge | ou | ow | tion |

reflec*tion*

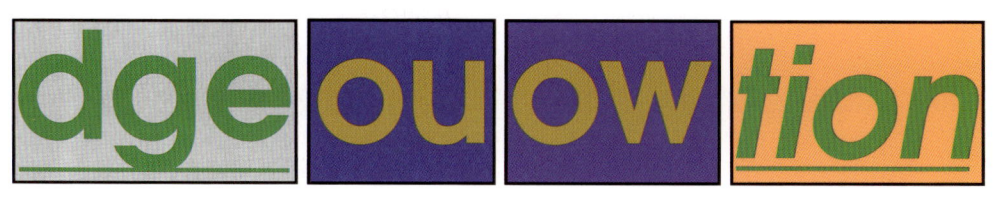

ridge

sound

| dge | ou | ow | *tion* |

Sentences!

A brown cow grazes near a bridge.

A cloud is drifting near a constellation.

Congratulations!
You are now ready to start reading books!

Appendix

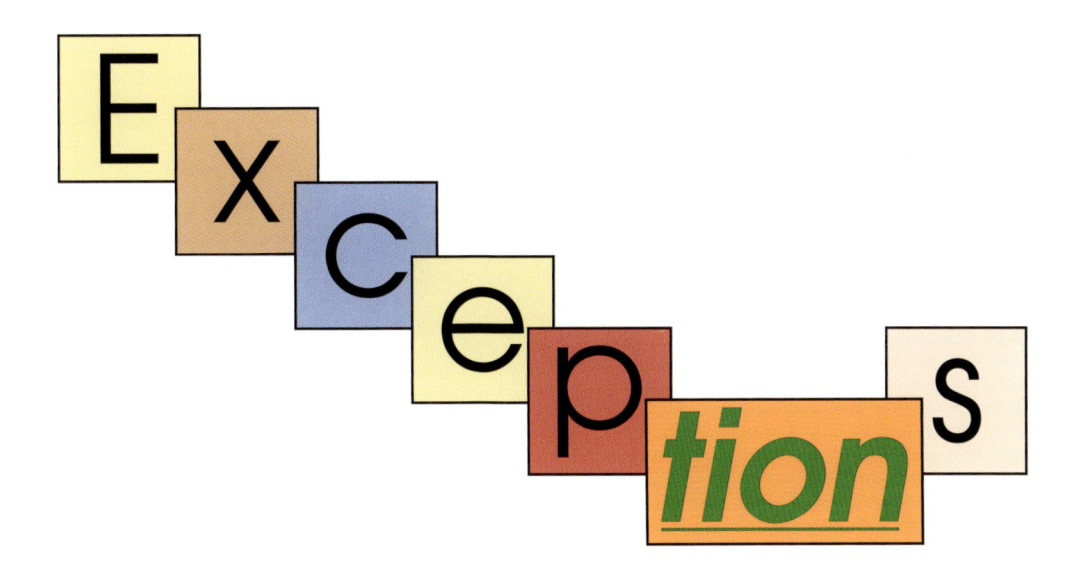

Exceptions

Once the phonetic sounds introduced herein are grasped, the student is encouraged to start reading beginner books. The new reader will undoubtedly encounter words with exceptions to these phonetic rules. In time, you may wish to teach some of these exceptions.

Some common exceptions are the soft "c" as in *center* and the soft "g" as in *gentle*. The letter combination "ie" is another common exception that takes the form of a long "e" sound as in *believe* or a long "i" sound as in *tried*. The suffixes "sion" and "ous" in *passion* and *stupendous* are among many other common exceptions your pupil may encounter.

This appendix includes a list of twelve sight words that can be added to the new reader's vocabulary. These sight words are among the 100 most common words in the English language and contain exceptions to the A**ar**dv**ar**k to Z**u**cchini **Ph**onetic Al**ph**abet. The phonetic alphabet is utilized to illustrate the proper pronunciation of these words. The phonetic pronunciations are implied through the use of a sound wave as shown at the top of this page. The new reader will find it easiest to simply memorize these common words.

Enjoy your reading journey!

Sight Words

by	b**i**
could	c**oo**d
do	d**oo**
should	**sh****oo**d
their	**th****a**ir
there	**th****a**ir
they	**th****a**y
to	t**oo**
who	h**oo**
would	w**oo**d
you	y**oo**
your	y**our**

Many thanks to the following individuals who provided valuable suggestions regarding this book by either testing the methodology with their children or offering their professional expertise. Their cumulative suggestions were all taken to heart to produce a better book.

Ambra Baldwin Hart
Thom Davis
Anne and Evan Gyura
Gemma May
Breanne Riesberg
Sai Suryanarayanan, Kata Beilin, and Mundo Suryan-Beilin
Andrew and Carter Webb
Mike and Ryan Ziegert